Let's Sightplay!

by Kathleen Massoud

D1548642

Book 2

ELEMENTARY LEVEL

Creative Solo Exercises to
Develop Sightplaying at the Piano

CONTENTS

The sequence of concepts in *Let's Sightplay!* is closely related to that used in *Piano Adventures*® by Faber and Faber (The FJH Music Company Inc.), and is one which can be successfully combined with most other methods.

Book 2 of *Let's Sightplay!* uses concepts presented in *Piano Adventures*® *Level 1*. It should be introduced to the student about midway through *Piano Adventures*® *Level 2A* (or later), since it generally is better to have students sightplay material a little easier than their current level.

*This book is dedicated to the Massachusetts Music Teachers Association,
with special thanks to Joan Garniss for her kind and generous support.*

A Note to the Teacher

Developing Sightplaying Skills

Sightplaying is a valuable skill which can be developed at the earliest stages of piano study. Proficiency in sightplaying will result from instilling the good habits of thinking ahead, keeping a steady beat, using correct fingerings, and recognizing intervals and other patterns.

Teachers will appreciate improved weekly lessons as students learn to pay closer attention to what is written on the page. When sightplaying is an integral part of weekly lessons, it becomes regarded as an attainable skill instead of one reserved just for "gifted" students.

Let's Sightplay! includes a variety of short exercises designed to drill the important elements of sightplaying, but always within a musical context.

How to Use This Book

Sightplaying refers to the first attempts at playing music that has never been tried before. It is not limited to just the first reading. Students should be encouraged to play exercises several times if they cannot accurately digest all the musical information on the first try.

The exercises in this book have been grouped into fourteen "Lessons," each with four different exercises. During the piano lesson, teachers may choose to hear any of the four exercises, with the remainder to be tried at home in order to save lesson time. It is important for students to understand that after each exercise can be played completely accurately, it is not to be practiced further. (Students may record in the book how many tries it takes to reach an accurate performance level.)

Motivating Students

Sightplaying should always emphasize accuracy as well as not stopping despite difficulties. One effective method to encourage students to value accuracy is by allowing them to earn points for accurate sightplaying.

In this book, points may be awarded according to how many tries it takes to play an exercise accurately. If the student is successful on the first try, that is worth 30 points; the second try, 20 points; and the third try, 10 points. (The teacher may use discretion to make these goals flexible and attainable by even the slowest student's best efforts.) Test exercises may include either new exercises or those assigned the previous week. If two exercises are tested, the student, at best, could earn up to 60 points. For every 100 points earned, it is suggested that the student may receive an incentive, such as a "composer stamp" or a special sticker.

Let's Sightplay! aims to make sightplaying into a challenging game, which in turn will make students respond with more concentration and effort.

A Note to the Student

Welcome to the world of sightplaying!

Here is a checklist you can use to help you sightplay better:

1. Always check the time signature and **count one measure aloud before starting.** (It's best to keep counting aloud as you play!)

2. What is the **first note** and **finger number** for the right hand? What is the **first note** and **finger number** for the left hand?

3. Do you see any tricky rhythms? Be on the lookout for ties and rests.

4. Are there places where both hands play together? **Always look ahead!**

5. Are there places where one hand plays two notes together? **Is the interval a 2nd, 3rd, 4th, or 5th?**

6. Are there any sharps or flats? Try not to miss any that occur more than once in the same measure.

7. Are there any slurs or staccatos? Try to remember the difference in sound between them as you play!

8. Do you see any note patterns that repeat? **It helps to find any measures that look alike.**

9. Do you see any dynamic marks? Following the dynamic marks will make the music sound more interesting!

10. Do you see any position changes? Plan your finger moves ahead of time.

In each lesson in this book, you will find some **"Sightplaying Hints"** which you should read **before** sightplaying the exercises. These hints will help you notice things in the music, so that you will sightplay more accurately.

4

Lesson One

1 Dialogue

Volleyball

SIGHTPLAYING HINT:
Choose a comfortable tempo (not too fast) so that you can play with a steady beat!

2 Sightplaying Chimes

Extra Credit: Metronome clicks
𝅗𝅥 = ☐   on every half note.

depress pedal   lift pedal

3 Sightplaying Chimes

Extra Credit: Metronome clicks
𝅗𝅥 = ☐   on every half note.

depress pedal   lift pedal

*All the Sightplaying Chimes in this book are to be played with the damper pedal down.

4A Theme

A Short Ride

SIGHTPLAYING HINT:
Remember to always count one measure aloud before playing!

4B Variation

Riding With The Hiccups

SIGHTPLAYING HINT:
On which beat of the measure are the staccatos ("hiccup notes") played?

4C Variation

Riding With A Kangaroo

SIGHTPLAYING HINT:
Almost every note has a staccato mark. Be prepared for the slur at the end!

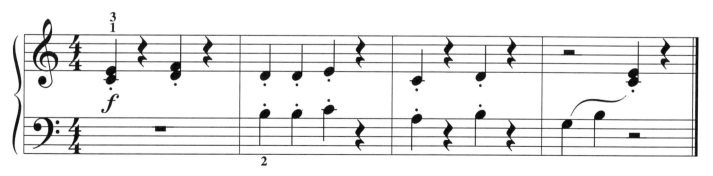

Lesson One total points* ☐

(Teacher: see "Motivating Students," page 2.)

Lesson Two

5 Dialogue

Pink Roses

SIGHTPLAYING HINT:
On which beat of the measure does the L.H. start? Be sure to count aloud!

6 Sightplaying Chimes

Extra Credit: Metronome clicks on every half note.

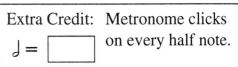

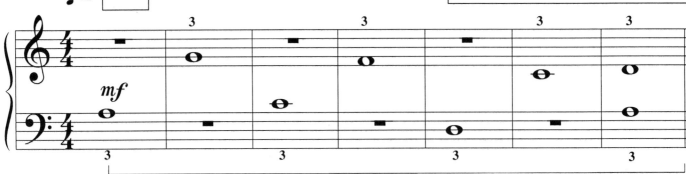

7 Sightplaying Chimes

Extra Credit: Metronome clicks on every half note.

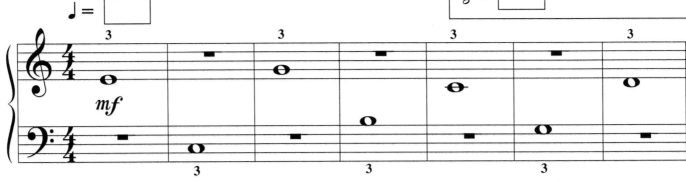

8A Theme

Smooth and Icy

SIGHTPLAYING HINT:
Look ahead to make the melody nice and smooth!

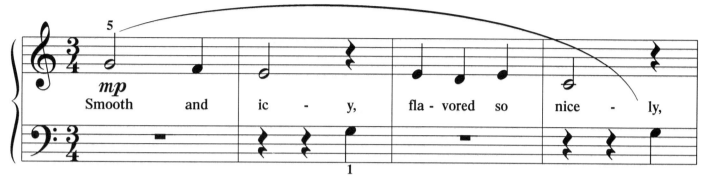

Smooth and ic - y, fla - vored so nice - ly,

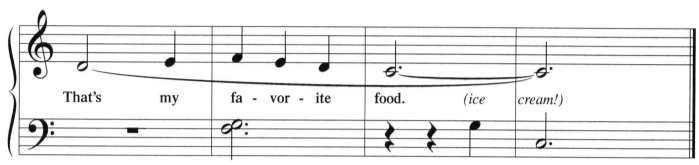

That's my fa - vor - ite food. *(ice cream!)*

8B Variation

Hot and Spicy

SIGHTPLAYING HINT:
The staccatos make this variation "hot and spicy!"

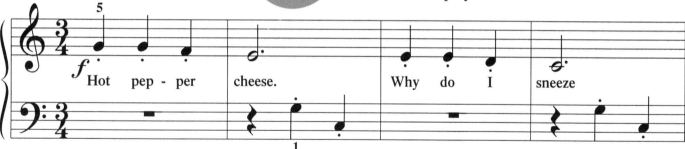

Hot pep - per cheese. Why do I sneeze

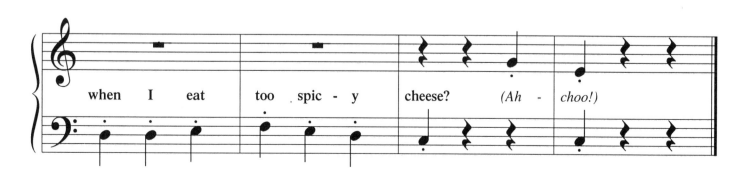

when I eat too spic - y cheese? *(Ah - choo!)*

Lesson Two total points ☐

Lesson Three

9 Dialogue

Bedtime Story

SIGHTPLAYING HINT:
Find all the intervals of a 4th
before playing.

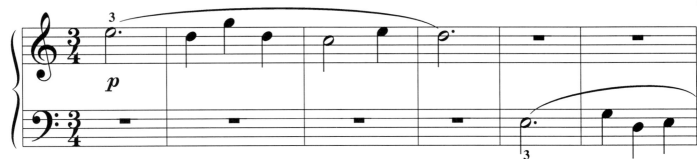

10 Sightplaying Chimes

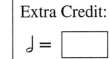

Extra Credit:

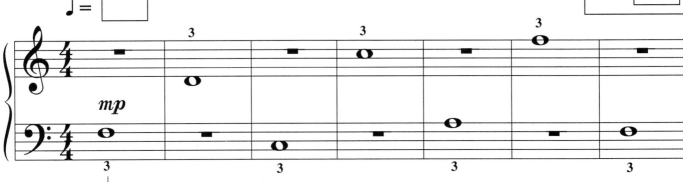

11 Sightplaying Chimes

Extra Credit:

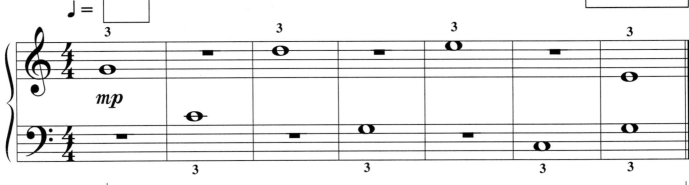

9

12A Theme

The Shepherd's Call . . .

SIGHTPLAYING HINT:
Can you find any matching measures
where the melody is exactly the same?

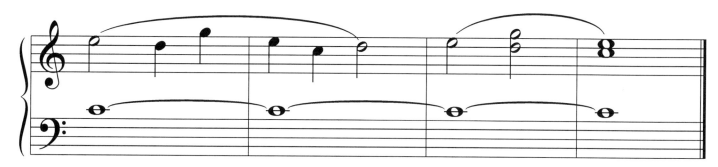

12B Variation

. . . The Sheep Follow

SIGHTPLAYING HINT:
How are the first lines of the
Theme and Variation alike?

Lesson Three total points ☐

10

Lesson Four

13 Dialogue

Bunny Hop!

SIGHTPLAYING HINT:
Name all the intervals where two notes
are played together.

14 Sightplaying Chimes

Extra Credit:

15 Sightplaying Chimes

Extra Credit:

16A Theme

Evening Stillness

SIGHTPLAYING HINT:
Notice the R.H. position. Recognizing the intervals will help you read more easily.

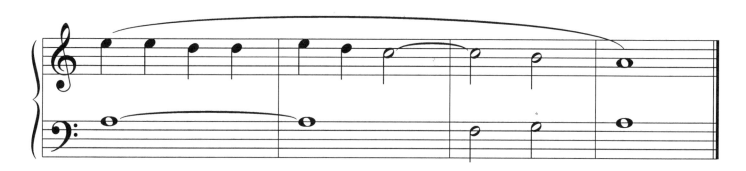

16B Variation

Crickets

SIGHTPLAYING HINT:
Count aloud, and be on the lookout for tricky rests!

Lesson Four total points [ ]

Lesson Five

17 Dialogue

Sunset

SIGHTPLAYING HINT:
Be sure to start with the correct fingering, then read the intervals carefully!

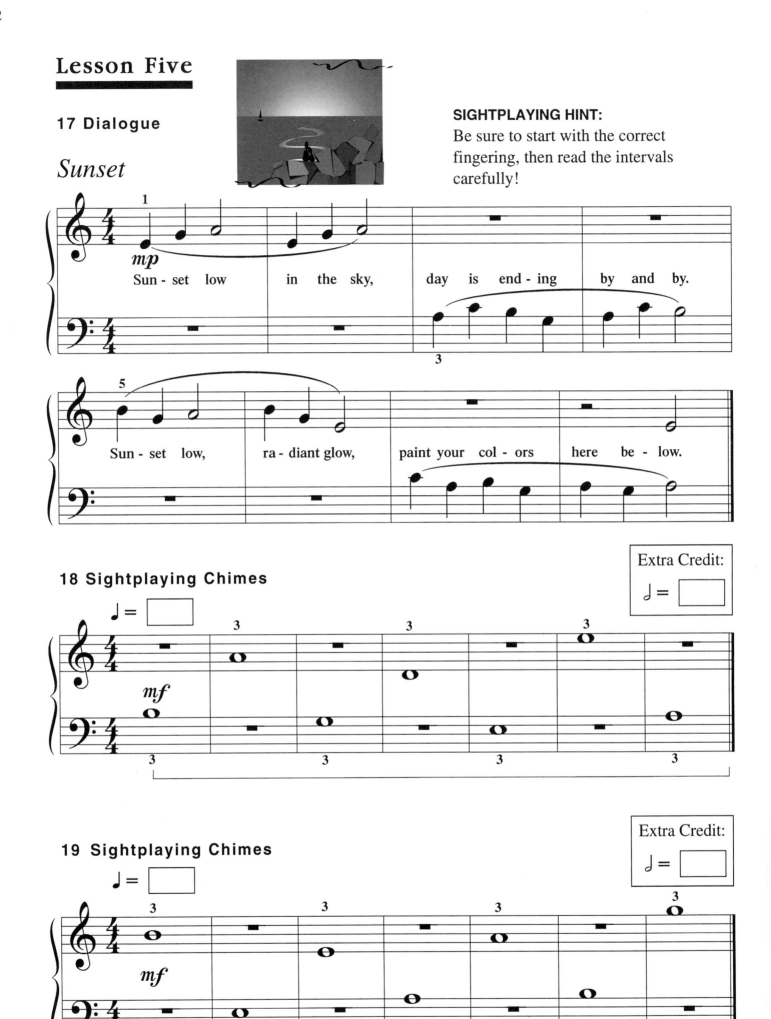

Sun - set low   in the sky,   day is end - ing   by and by.

Sun - set low,   ra - diant glow,   paint your col - ors   here be - low.

18 Sightplaying Chimes

Extra Credit:
♩ = ☐

mf

19 Sightplaying Chimes

Extra Credit:
♩ = ☐

mf

20A Theme

The Caterpillar

SIGHTPLAYING HINT:
Before playing hands together, notice the easy pattern of notes in the L.H.

20B Variation

The Butterfly

SIGHTPLAYING HINT:
Notice the L.H. notes in "The Butterfly" and "The Caterpillar" are the same!

Lesson Five total points ☐

FF1115

Lesson Six

21 Dialogue

Farewell

SIGHTPLAYING HINT:
Trust your fingers to play the correct intervals without looking down!

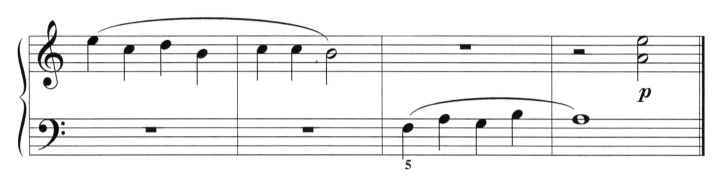

22 Sightplaying Chimes

Extra Credit:

$\quad$ = ◻

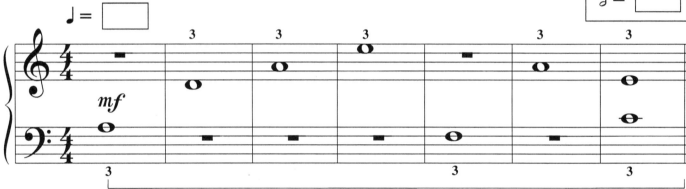

23 Sightplaying Chimes

Extra Credit:

$\quad$ = ◻

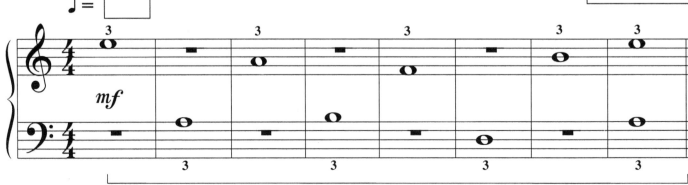

24A It's Your Move!

Raindrops I

SIGHTPLAYING HINT:
Find the starting note with the R.H. thumb, then find the note it moves to on the second line.

24B It's Your Move!

Raindrops II

SIGHTPLAYING HINT:
The circled fingerings will help you prepare for the position changes!

Lesson Six total points ☐

FF1115

16

Lesson Seven

25 Dialogue

Birthday Celebration

SIGHTPLAYING HINT:
Plan the fingerings you will use for the sharps in this piece.

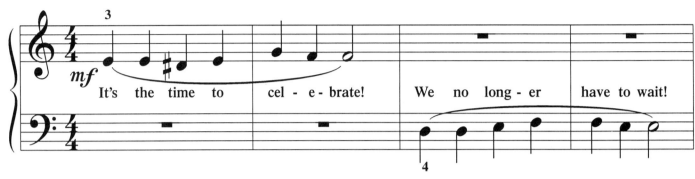

26 Sightplaying Chimes

Extra Credit:

♩ = ☐

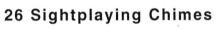

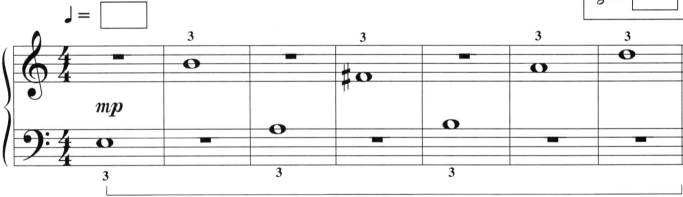

27 Sightplaying Chimes

Extra Credit:

♩ = ☐

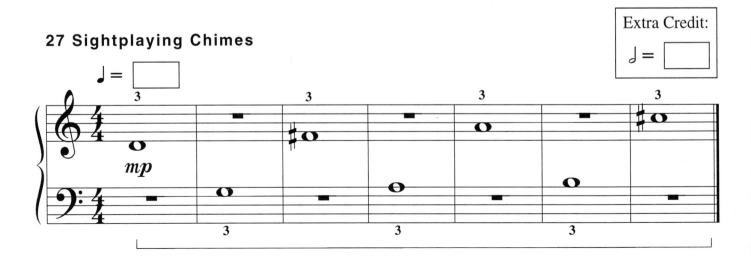

FF1115

28A Theme

March

SIGHTPLAYING HINT:
Try to keep your eyes on the music as you play.

28B Variation

Calypso

SIGHTPLAYING HINT:
Try tapping the rhythm before sightplaying. It's best to count this piece aloud!

Lesson Seven total points ☐

Lesson Eight

29 Dialogue

SIGHTPLAYING HINT:
Remember the difference in sound between slurs and staccatos as you play!

The Watermelon Song

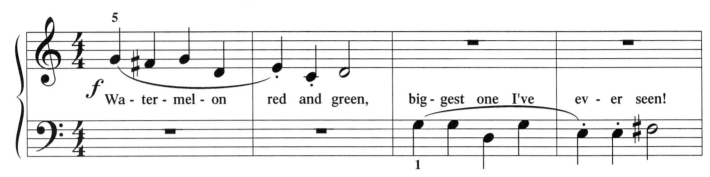

Wa - ter - mel - on red and green, big - gest one I've ev - er seen!

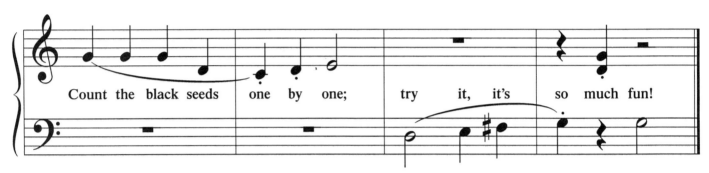

Count the black seeds one by one; try it, it's so much fun!

30 Sightplaying Chimes

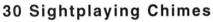

Extra Credit:

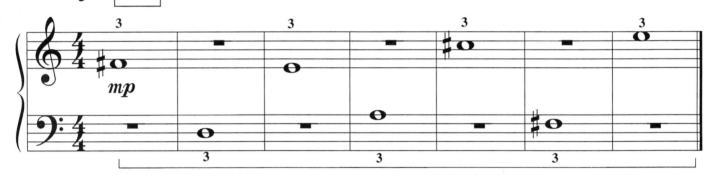

31 Sightplaying Chimes

Extra Credit:

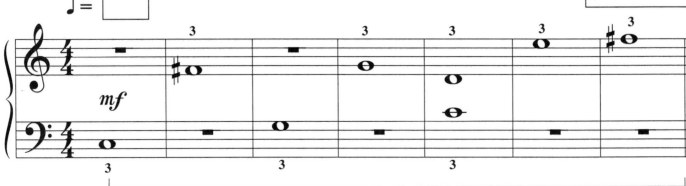

32A It's Your Move!

Daffodil Dreams I

SIGHTPLAYING HINT:
What note does the L.H. 2nd finger move to in measure 6? Be ready ahead of time!

32B It's Your Move!

Daffodil Dreams II

SIGHTPLAYING HINT:
Be sure to look ahead when coming to the end of a line!

Lesson Eight total points ☐

Lesson Nine

33 Dialogue

The Lonesome Prairie

SIGHTPLAYING HINT:
In this dialogue, one hand often has tied notes while the other hand plays the melody.

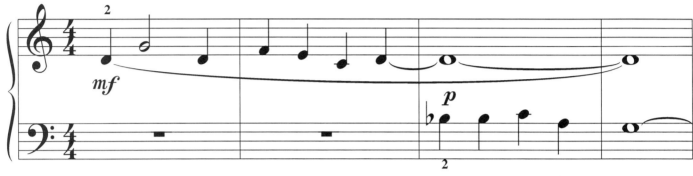

34 Sightplaying Chimes

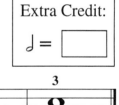

Extra Credit:

♩ = ☐

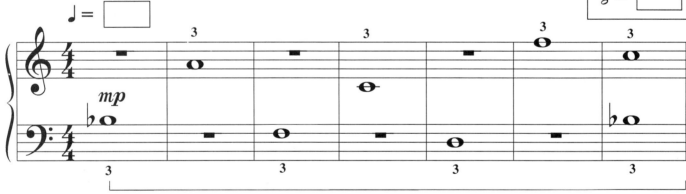

35 Sightplaying Chimes

Extra Credit:

♩ = ☐

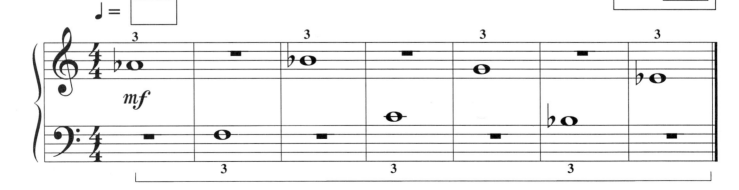

36A Theme

In A Japanese Garden . . .

SIGHTPLAYING HINT:
Can you find any matching measures
where the melody is exactly the same?

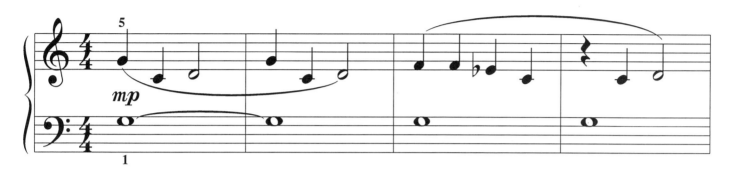

36B Variation

SIGHTPLAYING HINT:
Name all the intervals where one hand
plays two notes together.

. . . The Flowers Go To Sleep

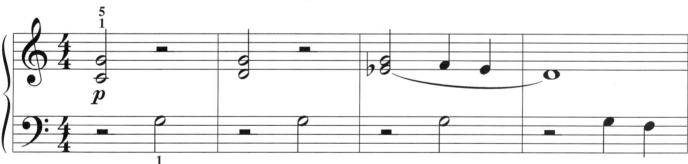

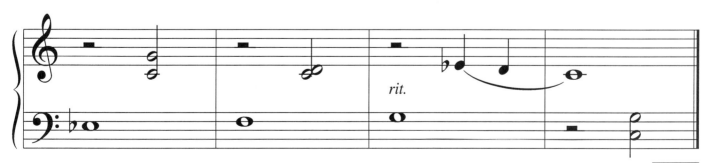

Lesson Nine total points

Lesson Ten

37 Dialogue

Snooping Around

SIGHTPLAYING HINT:
Find the measure where the same note is flatted more than once!

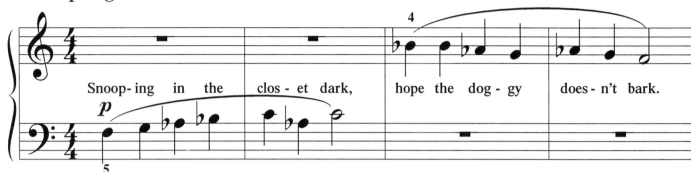

Snoop-ing in the   clos-et dark,   hope the dog-gy   does-n't bark.

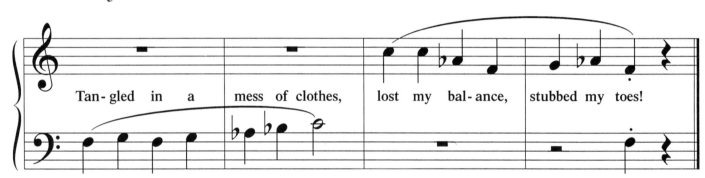

Tan-gled in a   mess of clothes,   lost my bal-ance,   stubbed my toes!

38 Sightplaying Chimes

Extra Credit:
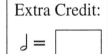

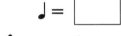

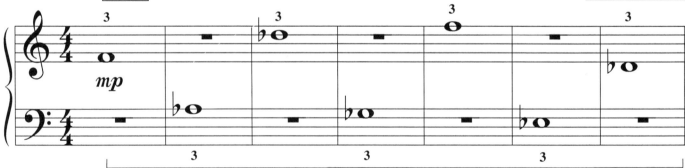

39 Sightplaying Chimes

Extra Credit:
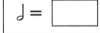

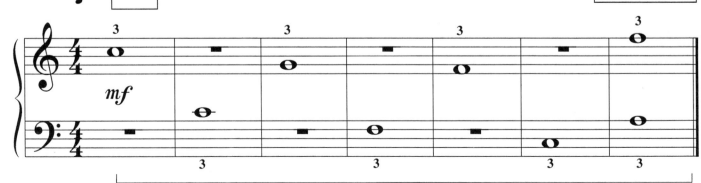

40A It's Your Move!

Buttercup Waltz I

SIGHTPLAYING HINT:
What note does the R.H. 2nd finger move to in measure 7? Look ahead and be prepared!

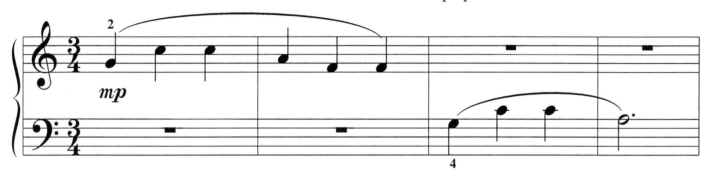

40B It's Your Move!

Buttercup Waltz II

SIGHTPLAYING HINT:
The L.H. starting position here is different. Plan ahead for finger moves!

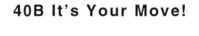

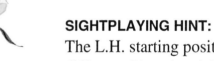

Lesson Ten total points ☐

Lesson Eleven

41 Dialogue

SIGHTPLAYING HINT:
How many 4ths can you find here?

Indian Trails

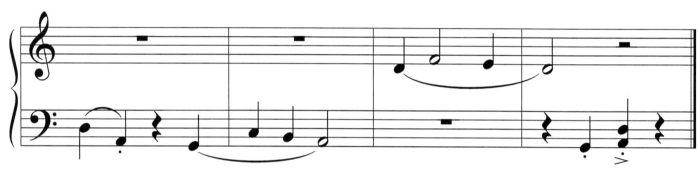

42 Sightplaying Chimes

Extra Credit:

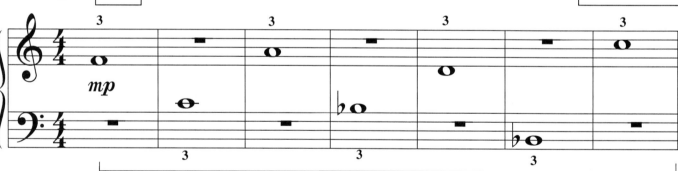

43 Sightplaying Chimes

♩ = ☐

Extra Credit:

♩ = ☐

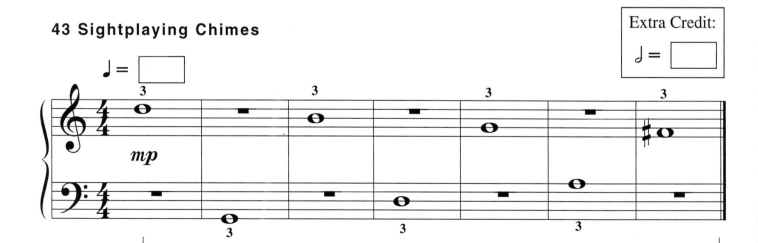

44A It's Your Move!

Indian Lullaby

SIGHTPLAYING HINT:
The R.H. changes position twice in "Indian Lullaby."

Lesson Eleven total points [ ]

Lesson Twelve

45 Dialogue

Ducklings

SIGHTPLAYING HINT:
Watch for repeated notes in the R.H.

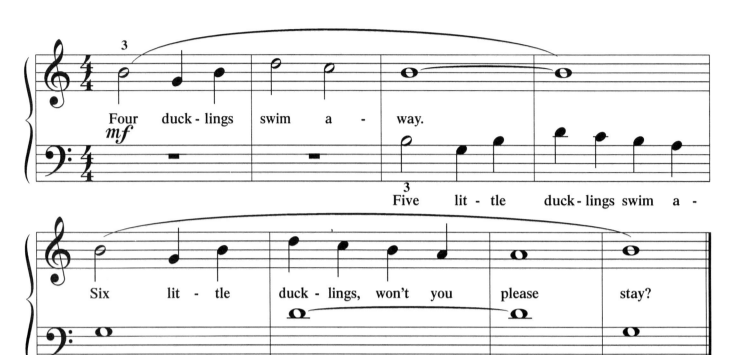

Four duck-lings swim a - way.

mf

Five lit - tle duck-lings swim a -

Six lit - tle duck - lings, won't you please stay?

way.

46 Sightplaying Chimes

Extra Credit:

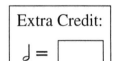

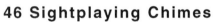

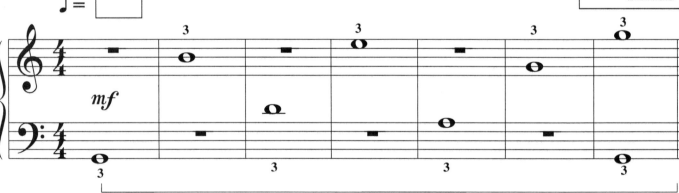

mf

47 Sightplaying Chimes

Extra Credit:

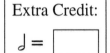

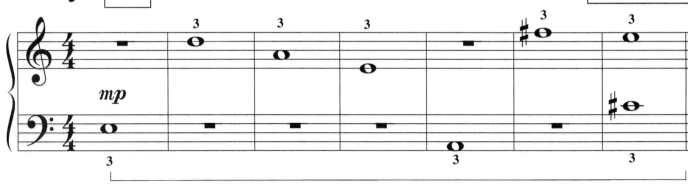

mp

48A Theme

Sing, Mister Bluebird

SIGHTPLAYING HINT:
Notice how many beats the first L.H. note is held.

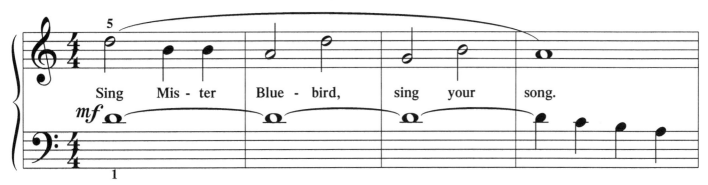

Sing   Mis - ter   Blue - bird,   sing   your   song.

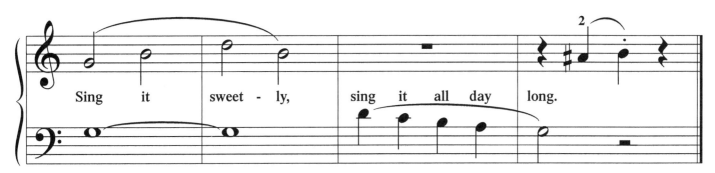

Sing   it   sweet - ly,   sing   it   all   day   long.

48B Variation

Mister Bluebird's (Funny) Song

SIGHTPLAYING HINT:
Compare the R.H. notes in the last measure (*Tweet!*) with the last measure of the Theme.

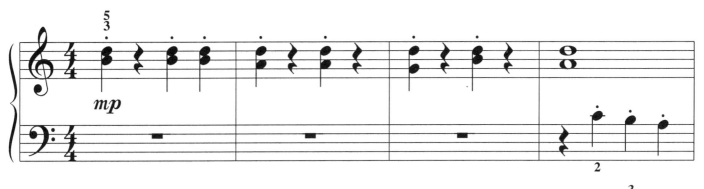

Tweet!

Lesson Twelve total points

Lesson Thirteen

49 Dialogue

Caravan

SIGHTPLAYING HINT:

On the keyboard, silently find the notes of measures 1 and 3, using the correct fingering.

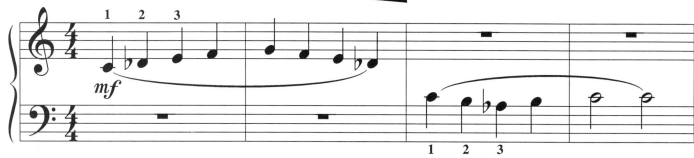

50 Sightplaying Chimes

Extra Credit:

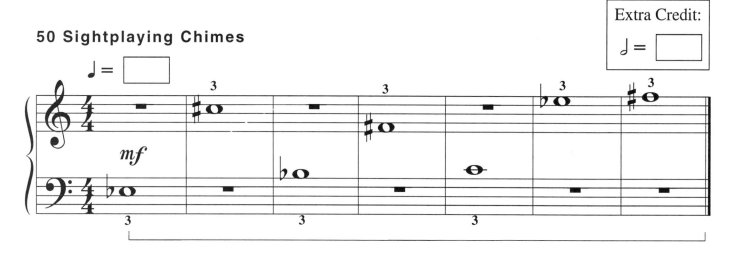

51 Sightplaying Chimes

Extra Credit:

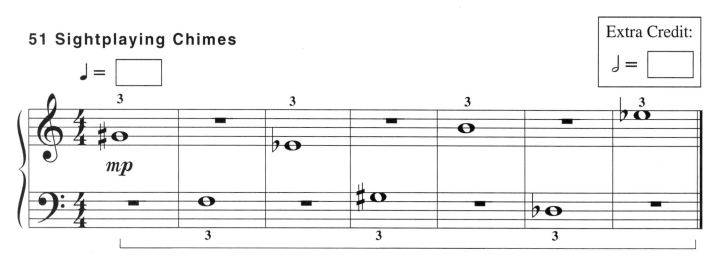

52A Theme

The Snake Charmer

SIGHTPLAYING HINT:
Compare the notes of measures 1 and 2
with the notes in measure 6.

52B Variation

The Charming Snake

SIGHTPLAYING HINT:
Silently play the sharp in measure 2 and
the flat in measure 7 with the correct
fingering.

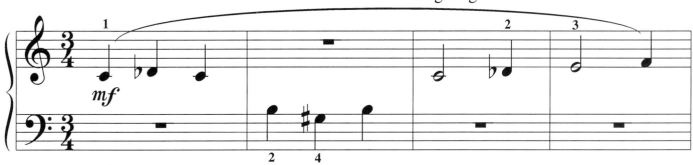

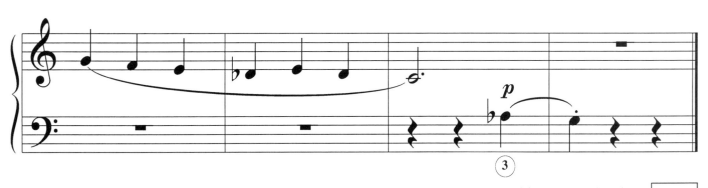

Lesson Thirteen total points [ ]

Lesson Fourteen

53 Dialogue

Alleluia

SIGHTPLAYING HINT:
Notice the different dynamic marks for each hand.

Sing al - le - lu - ia, sing____ al - le - lu - ia.

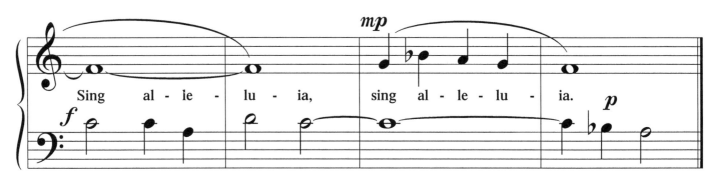

Sing al - le - lu - ia, sing al - le - lu - ia.

54 Sightplaying Chimes

Extra Credit:
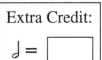

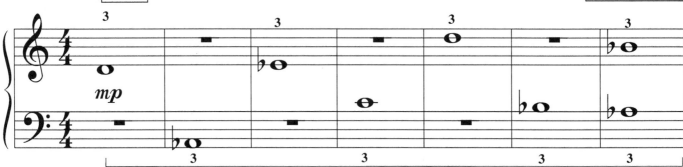

55 Sightplaying Chimes

Extra Credit:
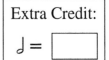

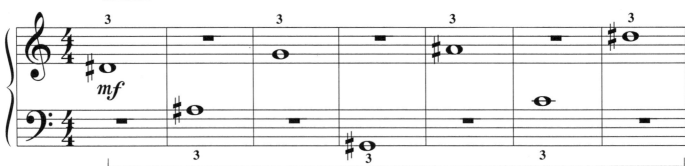

56A Theme

A Faraway Journey

SIGHTPLAYING HINT:
Point out all of the ties before playing.

56B Variation

The Return Home

SIGHTPLAYING HINT:
Trust your fingers and try not to look down except to find the L.H. position change.

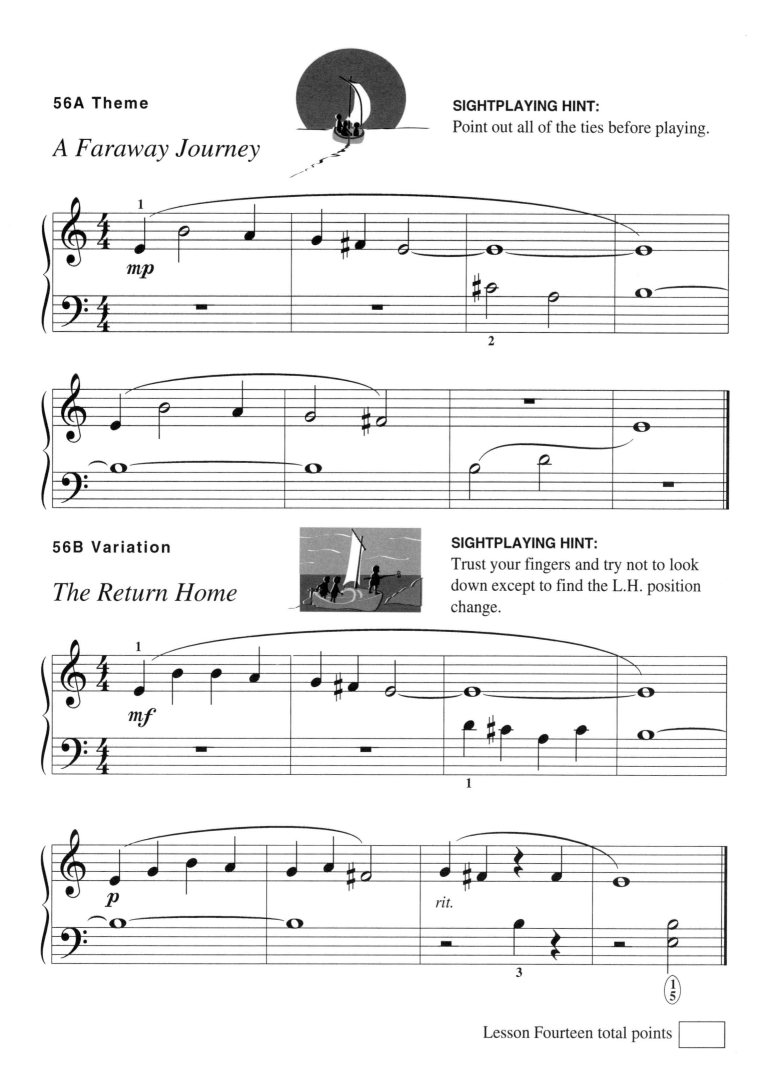

Lesson Fourteen total points ☐

Sightplaying Progress Report for Book 2

Accuracy:	Excellent	Good	Needs Improvement
Finds first note for each hand			
Plays correct rhythms			
Knows note locations on keyboard			
Knows note names on staff			
Recognizes intervals			
Uses good fingerings			
Notices dynamic marks			
Continuity (playing smooth and steady):			
Keeps eyes on music			
Looks and prepares ahead			
Keeps steady beat			
Keeps going after making a mistake			
Practice Habits:			
Follows sightplaying hints			
Counts one measure before starting			
Chooses good tempo (not too fast)			
Counts aloud while playing			
Uses metronome when assigned			

Teacher's Comments:

Congratulations to

_____

*for successfully completing **Let's Sightplay! Book 2***

Total earned points [   ]
(Lessons One – Fourteen)

_____
Date

_____
Teacher